AI POWERED CONTENT CREATION

Harnessing the Power of AI in Social Media

EDUARDO P CARABEO JR

Splat Communications

ISBN: 9798394742514

Cover design by: EP CARABEO JR
Generated Through Bing AI

This book is lovingly dedicated to my son Migs and my daughter Trixie. May your generation harness the power of AI in Social Media for the greater good of humanity.

"Where artificial intelligence meets the art of connection,
Unleashing the power of algorithms, shaping our social media reflection.
In this digital realm where humans and machines coexist,
Discover the secrets of crafting posts, where engagement persists.
Explore the fusion of data and creativity, a symphony of endless possibilities,
A journey through AI's influence on social media's realities.
Unlock the code to captivating content, igniting engagement's flame,
In this book's pages, AI and social media intertwine, forever changed."

CURATED BY JIGS CARABEO

CONTENTS

FOREWORD

It is with great pleasure that I write this foreword for the book "AI Powered Content Creation : Harnessing the Power of AI in Social Media." As an author of several books on Artificial Intelligence with over a decade of social media management experience, Jigs Carabeo captured the transformative power of artificil intelligence (AI) in the realm of social media platforms.

What sets this book apart is its ability to bridge the gap between the technical aspects of AI and the human-centric nature of social media. Jigs Carabeo elucidates complex concepts, making them accessible to readers from diverse backgrounds. The book does not only provide a panoramic view of the current state of AI in social media but also offers valuable insights to future trends and potential applications.

I have had the privildge of witnessing Jigs Carabeo's expertise and passion first hand, being the head of our department of Information and Communications Technology Office and I can attest to his deep commitment in unravelling the complexities of AI in social media. His unparalleled work ethic, meticulous research and attention to detail as well as his ability to articulate and simplify complex ideas makes this a valuable resource for anyone seeking to harness the power of AI for social media.

I wholeheartedly recommend "AI Powered Content Creation :

Harnessing the Power of AI in Social Media" a must-read for professionals, scholars and enthusiasts alike.

Mr. Jerald Mabuti
MA Public Administration
MA Information Technology
Marinduque State University

INTRODUCTION

In an era defined by connectivity, social media has evolved as a powerful force shaping the way we interact, communicate, and engage in the world around us. From sharing personal experiencing to building global communities, these platforms have become an integral part of our daily lives. But what lies beneath this seemingly simple interfaces?

Welcome to "AI Powered Content Creation : Harnessing AI in Social Media." In this book, we embark on a captivating journey that explores the convergence of artificial intelligence in social media, uncovering the profound impact on our digital landscape.

Artificial Intelligence, with its remarkable capabilities in data analysis, machine learnging and natural language processing, has transformed the way social media platforms operate. Algorithms guide our news feeds, suggest content, and target advertisements, while chatbots engage with us in real-time conversations. The marriage of AI and social media opens up a realm of possibilities, revolutionizing the way we create, consume and curate content.

Through these pages, we will delve in the intricate workings of AI in social media. We will unravel the secrets behind personal recommendations, discuss the nuances of sentiment analysis, and explore ethical considerations surrounding privacy and algorithmic bias. We will also discover the ways AI influence brand building, content strategy, influencer marketing, and social listening.

Whether you are a social media marketer, an inspiring influencer, a business owner or simply intrigued by the intersection of technology and human interaction "AI Powered Content Creation" offers a wealth of resources, valuable information, practical insights, and thought-provoking discussions. It is designed to empower you with the tools and understanding to navigate the ever-evolving social media landscape with confidence and creativity.

Welcome to AI Powered Content Creation.

Jigs Carabeo

PREFACE

Welcome the AI Powered Content : Harnessing the Power of AI in social media.

This book delves into the intersection of cutting-edge technology and the dynamic landscape of social media, where the power of Artificial Intelligence (AI) reshapes the way we connect, engage, and communicate with one another.

In this digital era, social media has become a part of our lives, offering endless opportunities to connect with people, share ideas and build communities. With the emergence of AI, these platforms have evolved into sophisticated ecosystems driven by algorithms, data analysis and automation.

AI Powered Content Creation is a comprehensive exploration of how AI transforms the landscape of social media. It offers unique perspective of harnessing the potential of AI to enhance one's social media presence, drive meaningful engagement, and optimize our digital interactions.

Through these pages, we embark on a journey that combines technological advancements with the art of social connection. This book goes beyond the technicalities and dives deep into the strategic and creative aspects of leveraging AI in social media. You will learn how to curate compelling content, build meaningful connections, optimize advertising campaigns, interpret analytics, and navigate the ethical considerations arising in this evolving digital landscape.

It is my hope that "AI Powered Content Creation" inspires you to embrace the fusion of technology and human connection. May it empower you to adapt, innovate, and thrive in the ever-evolving world of social media.

Jigs Carabeo

Empowering Content Creators: Harnessing the Power of AI in Social Media

CHAPTER 1:
INTRODUCTION TO
AI AND CONTENT
CREATION

Artificial intelligence (AI) has been making waves in a wide range of industries in recent years, and content creation is no exception. From generating ideas and conducting research to creating visual and written content, AI can be a powerful tool for streamlining and optimizing the content creation process.

But what exactly is AI, and how can it be used in content creation? Simply put, AI refers to computer systems that are able to perform tasks that typically require human intelligence, such as language processing, pattern recognition, and decision-making. These systems are able to learn from data and make predictions or decisions based on that learning, without being explicitly programmed to do so.

In the context of content creation, AI can be used in a variety of ways to help content creators work more efficiently and effectively. For example, AI can be used to generate ideas for blog posts, articles, or videos based on analysis of user behavior and interests. It can also be used to conduct keyword research and optimize content for search engines, or to create compelling visual content using algorithms that analyze images and other data.

One of the main benefits of using AI in content creation is the ability to automate certain tasks that would otherwise be time-consuming and labor-intensive. For example, instead of manually sifting through large amounts of data to identify trends or patterns, AI algorithms can quickly analyze and organize that data to provide insights that might be missed by humans.

Another benefit of AI in content creation is the ability to personalize content for specific audiences. By analyzing user behavior and preferences, AI algorithms can create customized content that is tailored to individual users, increasing engagement and driving conversions.

Of course, there are also some potential drawbacks and challenges associated with using AI in content creation. One concern is the risk of bias, as AI algorithms may reflect the biases of the data they are trained on. For example, if an algorithm is trained on data that is skewed towards a particular demographic, it may produce content that is biased towards that demographic as well.

Another challenge is the need to balance the use of AI with human creativity and input. While AI can be a powerful tool for streamlining certain tasks, it cannot replace the creativity and unique perspectives that humans bring to the content creation process.

Despite these challenges, however, the potential benefits of using AI in content creation are significant, and many content creators are already exploring the possibilities. Whether you are a blogger, marketer, or creative professional, AI can help you work more efficiently and effectively, freeing up time and resources to focus on the aspects of content creation that require human creativity and expertise.

In the following chapters, we will explore some of the specific ways that AI can be used in content creation, and provide practical guidance for incorporating AI tools into your workflow. We will also discuss some of the ethical considerations and challenges associated with AI in this context, and provide best practices for working with AI effectively.

AI is an exciting and rapidly-evolving field that has the potential to transform the way we create and consume content. By leveraging the power of AI, content creators can work more efficiently, personalize content for specific audiences, and gain valuable insights into user behavior and preferences. However, it is important to approach the use of AI in content creation with caution and to balance its use with human creativity and input. In the following chapters, we will explore the opportunities and challenges of AI in more detail, and provide practical guidance for incorporating AI into your content creation process.

CHAPTER 2: THE BENEFITS OF AI IN DIGITAL CONTENT CREATION

Artificial Intelligence (AI) has revolutionized the way content is created and consumed. In this chapter, we will discuss the benefits of AI in content creation and how it can help you as a digital content creator.

Increased Efficiency

AI can help speed up the content creation process by automating tasks such as research, writing, and editing. For instance, content creators can use AI-powered tools to generate topic ideas, research relevant keywords, and create headlines. This allows digital content creators to focus more on the creative aspects of content creation, rather than spending countless hours doing mundane tasks.

Improved Content Quality

AI tools can help enhance the quality of content by offering suggestions for grammar and style, as well as analyzing tone and sentiment. For instance, tools like Grammarly can help improve the quality of written content by suggesting corrections to grammar and spelling mistakes. Additionally, AI can help with content personalization by analyzing data about the audience, including their interests, search history, and social media behavior. This allows content creators to create more relevant and engaging content.

Better SEO

Search engine optimization (SEO) is crucial to the success of any content marketing strategy. AI tools can help with keyword research, competitor analysis, and even content optimization. For example, tools like Yoast can help content creators optimize their content for search engines by providing suggestions for meta titles and descriptions. This can help improve the ranking of the content on search engines, resulting in more traffic and higher engagement.

Enhanced Visuals

AI-powered tools can help with the creation of visuals, including images and videos. For instance, Adobe Sensei can automatically tag and organize images, making it easier for content creators to find relevant visuals for their content. Additionally, tools like Canva can help with the creation of graphics, such as social media posts and infographics. These tools make it easier for digital content creators to create high-quality visuals, even without graphic design experience.

Improved Audience Engagement

AI can help with audience engagement by analyzing user behavior and preferences, including their browsing and purchase history, social media interactions, and search queries. This information can be used to create personalized content that resonates with the audience. For example, Netflix uses AI to recommend movies and TV shows to its users based on their viewing history. Similarly, Amazon uses AI to recommend products to its customers based on their purchase history.

Streamlined Workflow

AI can help streamline the content creation process by automating tasks such as scheduling, publishing, and distribution. For instance, tools like Hootsuite can help content creators schedule social media posts in advance and track their performance. This can help save time and ensure that content is published consistently across multiple platforms.

Cost-Effective

AI-powered tools can help reduce the cost of content creation by automating repetitive tasks and minimizing the need for human intervention. This can be especially helpful for small businesses and startups that may not have the budget to hire a full-time content team. For example, tools like Canva offer a free version that allows users to create high-quality graphics without the need for expensive software or design skills.

Faster Analysis

AI can help with the analysis of content performance by providing real-time insights and data. For instance, tools like Google Analytics can provide detailed information about website traffic, user behavior, and conversion rates. This allows content creators to quickly identify what's working and what's not, and make necessary adjustments to their content strategy.

Improved Collaboration

AI-powered tools can help improve collaboration among content creators by facilitating communication, task delegation, and feedback. For example, tools like Asana can help teams manage projects, assign tasks, and track progress. This can help ensure that everyone is on the same page and that deadlines are met.

Competitive Advantage

Finally, AI can provide a competitive advantage by allowing content creators to stay ahead of the curve and adapt to changing trends and consumer behavior. For instance, AI can help identify emerging topics and keywords that are likely to be popular in the future. This can help content creators create content that is relevant and timely, and stay ahead of the competition.

In summary, AI offers numerous benefits when it comes to content creation. From increased efficiency to improved audience engagement, AI can help content creators create more effective and engaging content. However, it's important to remember that AI is not a substitute for human creativity and expertise. Rather, it's a tool that can help enhance the content creation process and help digital content creators achieve their goals in a more efficient and effective way. However, it is important to note that AI is not a substitute for human creativity and expertise. It is simply a tool that can help enhance the content creation process.

CHAPTER 3: THE ROLE OF AI IN IDEA GENERATION

Imagine this scenario: you are a content creator and you need a lot of ideas for your upcoming projects. It can be tough to come up with fresh and original concepts all the time, especially if you have deadlines to meet and limited resources. This is where AI can come in and help.

AI-powered tools can assist in idea generation by analyzing large amounts of data and identifying patterns and trends. By using these insights, content creators can come up with new ideas that are relevant to their audience and have a higher chance of success. Here are some ways in which AI can play a role in idea generation:

Content Recommendations

Social media platforms and streaming services like YouTube, Netflix, and Spotify use AI to recommend content to their users. For example, YouTube's algorithm suggests videos based on the user's watch history and engagement metrics, such as likes and comments. Netflix uses a similar approach to recommend movies and TV shows to its users based on their viewing history and preferences.

Content creators can use AI-powered recommendation systems

to get inspiration for their own content. By studying what their audience likes and engages with, AI can suggest new topics and themes that are likely to be well-received. For example, if a beauty blogger's audience engages with makeup tutorials more than skincare routines, AI can suggest more makeup-related topics for the blogger to explore.

Keyword Research

Keyword research is an essential part of SEO, as it helps content creators optimize their content to rank higher in search engine results pages (SERPs). AI-powered tools like Ahrefs, SEMrush, and Google Keyword Planner can help content creators with keyword research by identifying relevant keywords that people are searching for.

For example, a travel blogger planning a trip to Bali can use these tools to research popular keywords related to Bali tourism, such as "Bali beaches," "Bali culture," and "Bali food." By incorporating these keywords into their content, the blogger can increase their chances of ranking higher in SERPs and attracting more traffic to their website.

Sentiment Analysis

Sentiment analysis is a technique that uses AI to identify and understand the emotions and opinions expressed in a piece of text or social media post. By analyzing customer feedback, reviews, and comments, content creators can gain insights into what their audience likes or dislikes about their content.

For example, a food blogger can use sentiment analysis to analyze comments on their latest recipe post. If most of the comments are positive and express a desire for more similar content, the blogger can create more recipes in that style. On the other hand, if the comments are negative or express a desire for a different type of content, the blogger can pivot their content strategy accordingly.

Predictive Analytics

Predictive analytics uses machine learning algorithms to forecast future trends and behavior based on historical data. Content creators can use this technique to predict what topics or themes will be popular in the future and plan their content accordingly.

For example, a fashion blogger can use predictive analytics to forecast which fashion trends will be popular in the upcoming season and create content around those trends. By analyzing data on historical fashion trends, the blogger can predict which styles and colors will be in vogue and tailor their content to meet the anticipated demand.

Collaborative Filtering

Collaborative filtering is a technique that uses AI to recommend items based on the preferences of similar users. This can be applied to idea generation by analyzing the content that similar creators are producing and suggesting new ideas based on that.

For example, a cooking blogger can use collaborative filtering to analyze the content of other food bloggers and suggest new recipes or techniques that are currently popular. By studying what other successful food bloggers are doing, the blogger can come up with new and innovative ideas that are likely to be well-received by customers.

Natural Language Generation

Another area where AI can help with idea generation is through natural language generation (NLG). NLG is the process of using AI to produce human-like language. This can be useful for generating content like product descriptions, social media posts, and even entire articles.

For example, the Associated Press (AP) uses an NLG system to produce thousands of news articles each year. The system takes data from various sources and turns it into a readable news story. This allows the AP to quickly produce news content without the need for human journalists to write every article.

Predictive Analytics

Predictive analytics is the use of data, statistical algorithms, and machine learning techniques to identify the likelihood of future outcomes based on historical data. In content creation, predictive analytics can be used to identify what type of content will perform well in the future.

For example, a media company can use predictive analytics to identify which types of articles or videos are likely to go viral. This information can be used to inform content creation, ensuring that the company is producing content that is likely to be well-received by its audience.

AI can be a powerful tool in idea generation for content creation. Whether it's through analyzing data, generating language, or predicting future outcomes, AI can provide valuable insights and help content creators come up with new and exciting ideas. While it may never fully replace human creativity and ingenuity, AI can certainly complement it and make the creative process more efficient and effective.

CHAPTER 4: HOW TO USE AI FOR KEYWORD SEARCH

Keywords play a vital role in content creation as they help search engines identify and categorize your content. However, manually searching for the most relevant and effective keywords can be a time-consuming task. This is where AI-powered keyword search tools come in handy. In this chapter, we will discuss how to use AI for keyword search and provide examples of how it can improve your content creation process.

Understanding Keyword Research

Keyword research involves finding and analyzing the terms that people use to search for information on a particular topic. The goal is to identify the most relevant and high-traffic keywords to optimize your content for search engines. This can help increase your website traffic, improve your search engine ranking, and ultimately, drive more conversions.

Keyword research can be a challenging task, as there are millions of keywords to choose from. It requires an understanding of your target audience, the industry, and the competition. AI-powered keyword search tools can help simplify this process and provide you with accurate and actionable data.

How AI Can Help

AI-powered keyword search tools use natural language processing (NLP) algorithms to analyze large amounts of data and identify relevant keywords. They can provide insights into user search behavior, search volume, competition, and other metrics that can help you optimize your content for search engines.

One of the most significant advantages of using AI for keyword search is speed. AI-powered tools can analyze millions of keywords in seconds, saving you time and resources. They can also provide more accurate data than traditional keyword search methods, as they can analyze data from multiple sources and identify patterns that humans may miss.

AI-powered keyword search tools can also help you stay up-to-date with the latest trends and changes in search engine algorithms. As search engines continue to evolve, it's essential to keep your keyword strategy up-to-date to maintain a competitive edge.

Using AI for Keyword Research

To use AI for keyword research, you can start by selecting a reliable keyword research tool that uses AI algorithms. Some popular tools include Google Keyword Planner, SEMrush, Ahrefs, and Moz. These tools can help you identify relevant keywords based on your industry, competition, and target audience.

Once you have selected a tool, you can enter your seed keyword, which is the primary keyword or topic you want to rank for. The tool will generate a list of related keywords and provide metrics such as search volume, competition, and estimated cost per click

(CPC).

You can then use this data to refine your keyword strategy and optimize your content. For example, you can identify long-tail keywords, which are more specific and have lower competition. These keywords can help you rank for niche topics and attract highly targeted traffic to your website.

You can also use AI-powered tools to analyze your competitors' keywords and identify gaps in your keyword strategy. For example, you can use SEMrush to analyze your competitor's website and identify the keywords they are ranking for. You can then use this information to create content that targets those keywords or identify new keywords that your competitors may be missing.

Conclusion

AI-powered keyword search tools can help simplify the keyword research process and provide you with accurate and actionable data. They can help you identify relevant and high-traffic keywords to optimize your content for search engines, ultimately driving more traffic and conversions to your website. By using AI for keyword research, you can stay up-to-date with the latest trends and changes in search engine algorithms, giving you a competitive edge.

One of the advantages of using AI for keyword search is that it can help content creators identify long-tail keywords that are more specific and less competitive. Long-tail keywords are longer phrases that are more specific to a particular topic or niche, and they often have less search volume but also less competition. By targeting long-tail keywords, content creators can increase their chances of ranking higher in search results and attracting more relevant traffic to their website.

AI-powered tools like SEMrush and Ahrefs have features that allow content creators to discover long-tail keywords related to their niche. These tools analyze search data to identify common search queries and suggest related keywords that content creators may not have thought of. For example, if a content creator is writing about "digital marketing", a tool like SEMrush can suggest related long-tail keywords such as "digital marketing for small businesses" or "digital marketing trends in 2022".

Another way that AI can help with keyword search is through content optimization. AI-powered content optimization tools like MarketMuse analyze the content on a website and suggest changes to improve its relevance and search engine visibility. These tools analyze the content and identify gaps in the website's coverage of a particular topic, and suggest keywords and phrases that the content creator can add to the website to improve its relevance for search engines. By incorporating these suggested keywords into their content, content creators can improve their website's visibility and attract more organic traffic.

AI-powered keyword search can be a valuable tool for content creators looking to optimize their website for search engines and attract more relevant traffic. By using AI-powered tools to discover long-tail keywords and optimize their content, content creators can improve their website's visibility and reach a wider audience. However, it's important to remember that AI tools are a supplement to, rather than a substitute for, human expertise and creativity. By combining the power of AI with their own skills and knowledge, content creators can create high-quality content that engages and delights their audience.

CHAPTER 5: WRITING AND EDITING WITH AI

In today's digital age, writing and editing content has become easier and more efficient, thanks to the emergence of Artificial Intelligence (AI). With AI, writing and editing can be done faster and more accurately than ever before. In this chapter, we will explore the different ways AI can assist writers and editors in producing high-quality content.

Writing with AI

One of the most useful applications of AI in writing is in generating text. AI-powered writing assistants can help writers generate ideas, provide structure and coherence to their writing, and even suggest language and vocabulary choices.

For example, the popular writing tool Grammarly uses AI to suggest improvements to grammar, spelling, and style in real-time. The tool analyzes the text and provides suggestions for changes, which the writer can accept or reject. Other writing assistants like Textio use AI to help writers improve the effectiveness of their writing by suggesting language that is more likely to resonate with their target audience.

Editing with AI

AI can also be used to edit written content. Editing software like ProWritingAid and Hemingway Editor use AI algorithms to analyze written content and suggest changes that improve readability, clarity, and overall quality.

For example, ProWritingAid checks written content for grammatical errors, redundancies, and overuse of adverbs, among other things. It then suggests changes that the writer can implement to improve the quality of their writing.

Hemingway Editor, on the other hand, helps writers to simplify their language and improve readability by highlighting sentences that are difficult to read and suggesting alternative phrasing.

Translation with AI

Another application of AI in writing and editing is in translation. With AI-powered translation tools like Google Translate, writers and editors can quickly and accurately translate content from one language to another.

While AI-powered translation tools are not yet perfect, they can provide a good starting point for translation and save writers and editors a significant amount of time.

Content Analysis with AI

AI can also be used to analyze written content and provide insights into how it can be improved. Content analysis tools like MarketMuse use AI to analyze written content and suggest improvements to SEO, structure, and overall quality.

For example, MarketMuse can analyze a piece of content and suggest topics that could be added to improve the SEO of the content. It can also suggest structural changes that will improve the readability and overall quality of the content.

AI-Generated Content

Finally, AI can be used to generate content from scratch. While this technology is still in its infancy, there are already AI-powered content generators that can produce written content that is difficult to distinguish from content written by humans.

One example of this is GPT-3, a language generation model developed by OpenAI. GPT-3 can generate articles, essays, and even poetry that is difficult to distinguish from content written by humans. While the technology is not yet perfect, it is advancing rapidly, and it is likely that AI-generated content will become more prevalent in the future.

In conclusion, AI has transformed the way we write and edit content. With AI-powered writing assistants, editing software, translation tools, content analysis tools, and even AI-generated content, writers and editors can produce high-quality content faster and more efficiently than ever before. While the technology is not yet perfect, it is advancing rapidly, and it is likely that AI will continue to play an increasingly important role in content creation and editing in the future

Another useful AI tool in writing and editing is grammar checking. AI can scan through written content and identify grammatical errors and provide suggestions for corrections. This can be especially helpful for non-native English speakers who may struggle with complex grammar rules.

One popular grammar checker is Grammarly, which uses machine learning algorithms to analyze text and provide suggestions for grammar, spelling, and punctuation. It also provides suggestions for improving sentence structure and style.

In addition, AI can also be used for generating content summaries. This is particularly useful for content creators who need to summarize lengthy articles or reports. AI can quickly scan through the content and identify the most important information, presenting it in a concise summary.

One example of an AI tool for generating summaries is SummarizeBot. This tool uses natural language processing algorithms to identify key information in text and generate a summary. It can also translate text into different languages and generate audio summaries.

Lastly, AI can also be used for content planning and organization. AI tools can help content creators analyze data and identify trends to inform their content strategy. For example, AI can identify popular topics and keywords in a particular industry or niche, helping content creators tailor their content to what their audience is interested in.

One example of an AI tool for content planning is MarketMuse. This tool uses AI to analyze content and identify gaps in a website's content strategy. It also provides suggestions for new content topics and recommends improvements to existing content.

AI has proven to be a valuable asset in the world of content creation. From ideation to writing, editing, and organization, AI tools have streamlined the process and made it more efficient for content creators. By leveraging the power of AI, content creators can focus more on creating high-quality content that resonates with their audience.

CHAPTER 6:
CREATING ENGAGING
CONTENT WITH AI

In the world of digital content creation, engagement is everything. As creators, we strive to create content that will capture the attention of our audience, keep them interested, and ultimately drive them to take action. One way to achieve this is by leveraging the power of AI to create engaging content.

Here are some ways that AI can help you create more engaging content:

Content Personalization

One way to make your content more engaging is to personalize it for your audience. With AI, you can analyze your audience's behavior and preferences to create content that is tailored to their interests.

For example, Netflix uses AI algorithms to analyze viewers' watch history and recommend personalized movie and TV show recommendations. Similarly, Spotify uses AI to create personalized playlists based on users' listening habits.

Image and Video Optimization

Visual content is becoming increasingly important in the world of digital marketing, and AI can help you optimize your images and videos for maximum engagement.

For example, AI-powered tools like Adobe Sensei and Canva use machine learning algorithms to help you create eye-catching visuals that are optimized for different platforms and devices. These tools can also suggest edits to your images and videos to improve their composition, contrast, and color.

Natural Language Processing

AI-powered natural language processing (NLP) tools can help you create more engaging written content by analyzing and optimizing your language.

For example, tools like Grammarly and Hemingway Editor use NLP algorithms to analyze your writing and provide suggestions to improve readability, tone, and grammar. These tools can help you create content that is easy to understand and enjoyable to read.

Content Creation

AI can also help you create content from scratch. Tools like Articoolo and Wordsmith use natural language generation (NLG) algorithms to create written content automatically based on specific keywords and topics.

While these tools are not perfect and may require some editing, they can be useful for generating content quickly and efficiently. This can be especially helpful for content creators who need to produce a large volume of content on a regular basis.

Content Distribution

Finally, AI can also help you distribute your content more effectively. With AI-powered tools like Hootsuite and Sprout Social, you can schedule your social media posts for maximum engagement, analyze your performance metrics, and make data-driven decisions about how to optimize your content distribution strategy.

As content creators, our ultimate goal is to create content that engages our audience. With the help of AI, this process has become much easier and efficient. AI can assist in various aspects of content creation, such as generating ideas, crafting headlines, and even writing entire articles. In this chapter, we'll explore some of the ways AI can help us create engaging content.

Idea Generation

One of the biggest challenges in content creation is coming up with fresh and innovative ideas. AI-powered tools can help us generate ideas by analyzing trends, identifying gaps in the market, and even analyzing our own previous content.

For example, BuzzSumo is a tool that uses AI to analyze content across social media platforms and identify popular topics and trends. By using BuzzSumo, we can gain insight into what topics are resonating with our audience and use that information to generate new ideas.

Another example is Clearscope, an AI-powered tool that analyzes our existing content and suggests related topics and keywords we can use to expand our content. By using Clearscope, we can ensure our content is relevant, comprehensive, and engaging.

Crafting Headlines

The headline is the first thing our audience sees and is often the deciding factor in whether they'll click through to read our content. AI can assist us in crafting headlines that grab attention and pique curiosity.

For example, CoSchedule Headline Analyzer is an AI-powered tool that analyzes our headlines and provides feedback on how to improve them. The tool examines factors like word balance, length, and sentiment to suggest changes that will make our headlines more engaging.

Writing Assistance

AI can also help us with the actual writing process by suggesting improvements to our writing and even writing entire articles for us.

For example, Grammarly is an AI-powered tool that analyzes our writing for grammar, spelling, and punctuation errors. It also provides suggestions for improving clarity, conciseness, and tone. By using Grammarly, we can ensure our content is error-free and easy to read.

Another example is Articoolo, an AI-powered tool that can write entire articles based on a brief provided by the user. While the resulting articles may not be perfect, they can serve as a starting point for further refinement.

One example is OneSpot, an AI-powered content personalization platform that analyzes user data to create personalized content experiences. By using OneSpot, we can create personalized content recommendations, email campaigns, and even website experiences.

AI can be a powerful tool for creating engaging content. From idea generation to writing assistance and personalization, AI-powered tools can help us create content that resonates with our audience and drives engagement. As content creators, we should embrace these tools and use them to our advantage.

CHAPTER 7: DESIGNING VISUAL CONTENT WITH AI

In today's fast-paced digital world, where people have shorter attention spans, visual content is a critical element in capturing the attention of your target audience. It conveys messages and emotions in a much more effective way than text alone. However, not everyone has the skills or resources to create visually appealing content. This is where AI comes in. With AI-powered tools, even those with little to no design experience can create stunning visual content.

One of the most popular uses of AI in designing visual content is through image recognition and manipulation. This technology enables users to edit and enhance images with just a few clicks. For example, Adobe's Sensei AI can automatically identify and select the main subject in an image, making it easy to remove the background or add effects. Canva's Magic Resize feature also uses AI to automatically resize designs to fit various social media platforms, eliminating the need for manual adjustments.

Another significant use of AI in visual content design is in generating graphics and illustrations. AI-powered design tools such as Canva, Piktochart, and Adobe Illustrator can automatically generate designs based on the user's inputs. Users can choose from a wide range of templates, styles, and colors, and the AI algorithm will create a unique design based on their choices. This makes it easy for even non-designers to create professional-looking graphics for their marketing campaigns.

Personalized visual content is another area where AI can be extremely useful. For instance, Starbucks uses AI to create personalized drink recommendations for its customers. By analyzing their past purchases and preferences, the AI system can suggest new drinks tailored to their tastes. Similarly, Nike's Nike By You program allows customers to customize their sneakers using AI-powered design tools. They can choose the colors, materials, and even add personalized text, resulting in a unique and customized product.

Video content is also becoming increasingly popular in digital marketing, and AI can be used to enhance the video creation process. AI-powered video editing tools such as Magisto and Animoto can automatically edit footage, add music and effects, and create a professional-looking video in just a few minutes. This makes it easy for even small businesses to create engaging video content without the need for expensive equipment or editing skills.

One of the most innovative uses of AI in visual content design is in generating entirely new visuals. For example, DeepDream is an AI-powered tool that generates surreal and psychedelic images by analyzing and enhancing existing images. Another example is Google's AutoDraw, which uses AI to predict what the user is drawing and offers suggestions for a more professional-looking image. This technology can help designers come up with unique and creative visual content that can set them apart from their competitors.

AI is also being used to enhance the user experience of visual content. For instance, The North Face, an outdoor clothing brand, uses AI to help customers find the right products. By asking a series of questions, the AI system can narrow down the products that are most suitable for the customer's needs. This makes the shopping experience more personalized and engaging.

AI is revolutionizing the way we design visual content for digital marketing. From image recognition and manipulation to generating graphics and illustrations, AI-powered tools are making it easier than ever for non-designers to create professional-looking visual content. Personalization, video content, and entirely new visuals are also becoming increasingly important, and AI is helping businesses create unique and engaging content tailored to their audience. As AI technology continues to evolve, we can expect even more innovative ways to design visual content in the future.

CHAPTER 8: OPTIMIZING CONTENT FOR SEO WITH AI

Creating high-quality content is important for any digital content creator. However, even the best content won't be seen by anyone if it's not optimized for search engines. This is where AI comes in handy. In this chapter, we will explore how AI can help content creators optimize their content for SEO.

AI and SEO

SEO, or search engine optimization, is the practice of increasing the quality and quantity of traffic to a website through organic search engine results. In simple terms, SEO is the process of improving the visibility and ranking of a website or page on search engines such as Google, Bing, and Yahoo. With AI, content creators can improve their SEO strategies and increase their website traffic.

AI is capable of analyzing data, identifying patterns, and making predictions. This is especially useful for SEO, as it can help content creators understand how search engines work and what they look for in web pages. AI tools can analyze website content, user behavior, and search engine algorithms to provide insights and recommendations for improving SEO.

One of the most common uses of AI in SEO is keyword research. Keywords are the terms and phrases that people use to search for information on search engines. By identifying the right keywords, content creators can optimize their content to rank higher on search engine results pages (SERPs). AI-powered keyword research tools can help content creators identify the most relevant and effective keywords for their content.

Content Creation with AI

AI can also be used to create content that is optimized for SEO. For example, AI-powered content creation tools can generate content based on specific keywords, topics, or themes. This content can then be edited and refined by the content creator to ensure that it is high-quality, relevant, and optimized for SEO.

AI can also help content creators optimize their content for readability and user experience. For example, AI-powered tools can analyze the readability of content and make suggestions for improvements. They can also analyze user behavior on a website and provide recommendations for improving the user experience.

Content Optimization with AI

Once content is created, it's important to optimize it for SEO. This involves making sure that the content is easily discoverable by search engines and that it meets the criteria for ranking high on SERPs. AI can help content creators optimize their content in several ways.

First, AI can analyze website content and provide recommendations for improving it. For example, AI-powered content optimization tools can identify duplicate content, broken links, missing metadata, and other issues that can affect SEO.

They can also analyze the content structure, use of headings, and other factors to provide recommendations for improving the content's visibility and ranking.

Second, AI can help content creators optimize their content for voice search. Voice search is becoming increasingly popular, and content creators need to optimize their content accordingly. AI-powered tools can analyze user queries and provide recommendations for creating content that is optimized for voice search.

Third, AI can help content creators optimize their content for local SEO. Local SEO is the process of optimizing content for location-based searches. AI-powered tools can analyze local search trends and provide recommendations for creating content that is relevant and useful for local audiences.

AI is a powerful tool for content creators looking to optimize their content for SEO. With AI-powered tools for keyword research, content creation, and content optimization, content creators can improve their SEO strategies and increase their website traffic. By utilizing AI in their content creation process, content creators can create high-quality, relevant, and optimized content that ranks high on search engine results pages.

CHAPTER 9: PERSONALIZATION WITH AI: CREATING CUSTOMIZED CONTENT

In the digital age, personalization has become an increasingly important aspect of content creation. Consumers have come to expect personalized experiences across all channels, and this includes the content they consume. As a content creator, it is important to understand how AI can be used to create customized content that speaks directly to your audience.

What is Personalization with AI?

Personalization with AI refers to the use of artificial intelligence to tailor content to individual users based on their preferences, behavior, and other relevant data. This can include everything from product recommendations to customized email campaigns and website content. Personalization with AI allows you to create a more relevant and engaging experience for your audience, which can lead to increased customer loyalty and conversion rates.

How Does AI Enable Personalization?

AI is able to enable personalization by analyzing large amounts of data about your audience and their behavior. This can include demographic information, search history, purchase history, and more. Using machine learning algorithms, AI can identify patterns and make predictions about what content each individual user is most likely to engage with.

One example of AI-enabled personalization is Netflix. Netflix uses machine learning algorithms to analyze user data, including watch history and search queries, to recommend content that each individual user is most likely to enjoy. This has led to increased user engagement and loyalty, as users feel like they are getting a more personalized experience.

Another example of AI-enabled personalization is Amazon. Amazon uses AI to personalize the shopping experience for each individual user, based on their search history and purchase history. This includes product recommendations, customized email campaigns, and personalized website content. This has led to increased conversion rates and customer loyalty.

How Can You Use AI for Personalization?

There are several ways that you can use AI for personalization in your content creation. One of the most common ways is through email campaigns. Using AI, you can create customized email campaigns that are tailored to each individual user, based on their behavior and preferences. This can include personalized product recommendations, customized subject lines, and more.

Another way to use AI for personalization is through website content. By analyzing user data, you can personalize the content that each user sees on your website, based on their behavior and preferences. This can include personalized product recommendations, customized landing pages, and more.

Finally, you can use AI for personalization in your social media marketing. By analyzing user data, you can create customized social media campaigns that are tailored to each individual user, based on their behavior and preferences. This can include personalized product recommendations, customized ad copy, and more.

Benefits of Personalization with AI

There are several benefits to using AI for personalization in your content creation. One of the biggest benefits is increased customer loyalty. By creating a more personalized experience for your audience, you can build stronger relationships with your customers and increase their loyalty to your brand.

Another benefit of personalization with AI is increased conversion rates. By tailoring your content to each individual user, you can create a more engaging experience that is more likely to lead to conversions. This can lead to increased sales and revenue for your business.

Finally, personalization with AI can help you to save time and resources. By automating the personalization process, you can create customized content at scale, without the need for manual intervention. This can help you to save time and resources, while still creating a personalized experience for your audience.

Personalization with AI is an important aspect of content creation in the digital age. By using AI to create customized content, you can create a more relevant and engaging experience for your audience, which can lead to increased customer loyalty and conversion rates. Whether you are creating email campaigns, website content, or social media marketing, there are many ways that you can use AI to personalize your digital content.

CHAPTER 10:
CREATING VIDEO
AND AUDIO
CONTENT WITH AI

In today's digital age, video and audio content are becoming more and more prevalent. From podcasts to YouTube videos, creating high-quality video and audio content has become a critical component of content creation. However, producing high-quality video and audio content can be time-consuming, expensive, and difficult. This is where AI comes in. AI can help content creators produce high-quality video and audio content quickly, easily, and inexpensively. In this chapter, we will explore how AI can be used to create video and audio content and how content creators can take advantage of this technology to improve their content creation process.

AI and Video Content Creation

AI can be used in several ways to create high-quality video content. One way is through the use of automated video editing tools. These tools use AI algorithms to analyze footage and create a polished video. Automated video editing tools can perform tasks such as trimming footage, adding music and sound effects, and color grading. These tools can save content creators a significant amount of time and effort and produce high-quality videos that look like they were edited by a professional.

Another way AI can be used to create video content is through the use of virtual sets. Virtual sets are computer-generated backgrounds that can be used instead of traditional sets. These sets can be created using AI algorithms and can be customized to fit the needs of the content creator. Virtual sets are often used in news broadcasts and other live events, where traditional sets may be impractical or expensive to use.

AI and Audio Content Creation

AI can also be used to create high-quality audio content. One way is through the use of automated audio editing tools. These tools can be used to remove background noise, adjust volume levels, and add effects such as reverb and echo. Automated audio editing tools can save content creators a significant amount of time and effort and produce high-quality audio that sounds like it was edited by a professional.

Another way AI can be used to create audio content is through the use of text-to-speech technology. Text-to-speech technology uses AI algorithms to convert written text into spoken words. This technology can be used to create podcasts, audiobooks, and other types of audio content quickly and easily. Text-to-speech technology can save content creators a significant amount of time and effort and produce high-quality audio that sounds like it was recorded by a professional voice actor.

AI and Content Personalization

AI can also be used to personalize video and audio content. Personalization involves creating content that is tailored to the individual viewer or listener. This can be done using AI algorithms that analyze user data such as viewing history, location, and preferences. Content creators can use this data to create personalized content that is more engaging and relevant to the individual viewer or listener.

For example, a streaming service can use AI algorithms to analyze a user's viewing history and recommend content that is similar to what the user has previously watched. This can lead to a more engaging and personalized viewing experience for the user. Similarly, a podcast platform can use AI algorithms to analyze a listener's listening history and recommend podcasts that are relevant to the listener's interests.

AI technology has revolutionized the content creation industry, making it easier and more efficient for content creators to produce high-quality video and audio content. By using automated editing tools, virtual sets, and text-to-speech technology, content creators can create professional-looking videos and audio content quickly and easily. Additionally, AI algorithms can be used to personalize content, making it more engaging and relevant to individual viewers and listeners. As AI technology continues to advance, we can expect to see even more innovation in the content creation industry.

CHAPTER 11:
UNDERSTANDING
USER BEHAVIOR
WITH AI

The success of any digital content relies heavily on its ability to attract and retain users. Understanding user behavior is key to achieving this. Thanks to advancements in artificial intelligence (AI), it has become easier than ever to gather and analyze data about user behavior. In this chapter, we'll explore how AI can help digital content creators gain insights into user behavior and how to leverage these insights to improve user engagement.

AI-powered User Behavior Tracking

One of the primary benefits of using AI to track user behavior is the ability to gather and analyze large amounts of data in real-time. This data can include everything from user demographics to their browsing behavior on a website. AI algorithms can then process this data to generate insights that can help digital content creators understand how users are interacting with their content.

For example, AI algorithms can track how long users are spending on a particular page, what sections of a page they are interacting with the most, and how they are navigating through the website.

This information can be used to identify areas where users are losing interest or getting confused, which can help content creators make improvements to the content and website design.

Personalized Content Recommendations

Another way that AI can help digital content creators is by providing personalized content recommendations to users. By analyzing user behavior data, AI algorithms can identify patterns in the types of content that users are most interested in. This information can then be used to provide personalized recommendations for content that users are likely to find engaging.

For example, if a user frequently reads articles about technology, an AI-powered content recommendation engine can suggest similar articles or content related to technology. By providing users with personalized recommendations, digital content creators can increase user engagement and build a more loyal audience.

Improving User Engagement with Chatbots

Chatbots are another example of how AI can be used to improve user engagement. By leveraging natural language processing (NLP) algorithms, chatbots can interact with users in a conversational manner, providing personalized assistance and answering questions in real-time.

Chatbots can be integrated into websites and messaging apps, providing users with an easy and convenient way to access information and support. For example, a chatbot on a website can help users find the information they need, such as answers to frequently asked questions or product information.

Predictive Analytics for User Behavior

Predictive analytics is another area where AI can help digital content creators understand user behavior. By analyzing user data, AI algorithms can identify patterns and make predictions about how users are likely to behave in the future. This information can then be used to make informed decisions about how to improve user engagement.

For example, predictive analytics can help digital content creators identify which types of content are likely to be most popular among users in the future. This information can be used to create more of the same type of content, which can help to keep users engaged and coming back for more.

AI has the potential to revolutionize the way that digital content creators understand and engage with their audiences. By leveraging AI-powered user behavior tracking, personalized content recommendations, chatbots, and predictive analytics, content creators can gain a deeper understanding of how users are interacting with their content and make data-driven decisions to improve user engagement. As AI continues to evolve, it will be exciting to see how it can be used to create even more engaging and personalized digital content.

CHAPTER 12: PREDICTIVE ANALYTICS AND CONTENT CREATION

In the world of digital content creation, there's always a need for fresh and exciting content. But with so much content available online, it can be challenging to stand out from the crowd. That's where predictive analytics comes in.

Predictive analytics is a method that uses data, statistical algorithms, and machine learning techniques to identify the likelihood of future outcomes based on historical data. In the context of content creation, predictive analytics can help content creators understand what their audience is interested in and what they are likely to engage with in the future.

There are various ways to use predictive analytics in content creation. One way is to analyze data from social media platforms to identify trends and patterns in user behavior. By understanding what type of content is resonating with your audience, you can create similar content that is more likely to be successful.

Another way to use predictive analytics in content creation is to analyze data from your website or blog. By understanding which pages or posts are generating the most traffic, you can create more content that is similar in style or topic. You can also use this data to identify which topics are not performing well and adjust your content strategy accordingly.

Predictive analytics can also help you optimize your content for search engines. By analyzing keyword data and search engine rankings, you can identify which keywords are most relevant to your audience and which ones are likely to generate the most traffic. This information can be used to create content that is more likely to rank well in search engine results pages (SERPs).

Another way to use predictive analytics in content creation is to identify which content formats are most popular with your audience. For example, if your audience prefers video content, you can focus on creating more video content. If they prefer long-form articles, you can create more articles that are over 1,500 words.

One of the key benefits of using predictive analytics in content creation is that it can help you save time and resources. By identifying which topics and formats are most likely to be successful, you can focus your efforts on creating content that is more likely to resonate with your audience.

Another benefit is that predictive analytics can help you create more personalized content. By analyzing data on individual user behavior, you can create content that is tailored to their interests and preferences. This can help increase engagement and build stronger relationships with your audience.

However, it's important to note that predictive analytics is not a silver bullet for content creation. It's just one tool that can help content creators make more informed decisions. It's still important to have a solid understanding of your audience and to create content that is high-quality and relevant.

Predictive analytics is a powerful tool that can help content creators create more engaging and effective content. By analyzing data on user behavior, trends, and patterns, you can make more informed decisions about what content to create and how to optimize it for maximum impact. As AI and machine learning continue to advance, predictive analytics will become even more valuable for content creation.

CHAPTER 13: ETHICAL CONSIDERATIONS OF AI IN CONTENT CREATION

As AI technology continues to evolve and shape the way we create and consume content, it is important to consider the ethical implications that arise. AI has the potential to revolutionize the way we create and distribute content, but there are also significant concerns surrounding its use.

One of the most pressing ethical considerations is the potential for AI to be used to create fake news and propaganda. As AI becomes more sophisticated, it becomes easier to manipulate audio and video content to create convincing fake news stories. This could have serious consequences for democracy and the public's trust in media.

Another ethical consideration is the potential for AI to perpetuate bias and discrimination. AI algorithms are only as unbiased as the data they are trained on, and if that data is biased, the algorithm will be too. This can result in discriminatory outcomes in areas such as hiring, lending, and criminal justice. If the data is biased or discriminatory, the AI will also be biased or discriminatory. This can have serious consequences in content creation, such as perpetuating harmful stereotypes or excluding certain groups of people. It is important to ensure that the data used to train AI is diverse and representative of all groups.

It is also important to consider the impact that AI will have on employment in the content creation industry. While AI has the potential to increase efficiency and productivity, it also has the potential to replace human workers. This could result in widespread job loss and economic disruption. AI has the potential to automate many tasks involved in content creation, which could lead to job displacement. It is important to consider the impact of AI on the workforce and take steps to mitigate any negative effects.

Consider privacy and security. AI relies on large amounts of data to function, which can include personal information. It is crucial to protect this data and ensure that it is not being misused or accessed without permission. Additionally, AI-generated content may also contain personal information, such as facial recognition or location data, which must also be protected.

The need to be transparent. It is important to be transparent about the use of AI in content creation. This includes disclosing when AI is being used to create content and how it is being used. It also includes being transparent about any biases or limitations in the AI's capabilities.

In addition to these concerns, there are also broader ethical considerations surrounding the use of AI in society. AI has the potential to exacerbate existing power imbalances and create new ones, and it is important to ensure that it is used in a way that promotes fairness, equality, and social justice.

The issue of accountability. As with any technology, there must be accountability for the use of AI in content creation. This includes holding creators and users of AI-generated content responsible for any harm caused by the content. It also includes ensuring that there are processes in place to address any issues or complaints related to AI-generated content.

Intellectual Property Issues should be considered seriously. AI-generated content raises questions about ownership and intellectual property. Who owns the content created by AI? How can creators protect their original work from being copied or used without permission? These are important questions that must be addressed.

To address these ethical considerations, it is important to have clear guidelines and regulations surrounding the use of AI in content creation. This includes ensuring that algorithms are transparent, explainable, and accountable, and that they are trained on diverse and unbiased datasets.

It is also important to encourage collaboration between AI developers, content creators, and other stakeholders to ensure that the technology is being used in a way that benefits society as a whole. This includes investing in research and development of AI that is designed to address societal challenges and promote social good.

While AI has the potential to transform the content creation industry in many positive ways, it is important to consider the ethical implications that arise. By addressing these concerns through clear guidelines and collaboration between stakeholders, we can ensure that AI is used in a way that benefits everyone. AI is complex and can have unintended consequences. It is important to consider the potential negative effects of AI-generated content, such as spreading misinformation or promoting harmful content.

By considering these ethical considerations, we can ensure that AI is used in a responsible and ethical manner in content creation.

CHAPTER 14: HOW TO EVALUATE AI TOOLS FOR CONTENT CREATION

Artificial intelligence (AI) tools have revolutionized the way we create content. From generating ideas to writing articles, AI has the ability to make our lives easier and more efficient. However, with so many AI tools available on the market, it can be challenging to choose the right one for your specific needs. In this chapter, we will discuss how to evaluate AI tools for content creation.

Firstly, it is essential to identify your content creation goals. What type of content are you looking to create? Are you looking to generate ideas, write articles, or produce videos? Once you have identified your goals, you can then narrow down your search for the appropriate AI tools.

Next, evaluate the accuracy of the AI tools. It is essential to ensure that the AI tool you choose can accurately create the type of content you need. For example, if you're looking to generate ideas, ensure that the AI tool can generate creative and unique ideas. If you're looking to write articles, ensure that the AI tool can produce high-quality and engaging content.

Another important consideration is the user-friendliness of the AI tool. You want an AI tool that is easy to use and understand, with a user interface that is intuitive and straightforward. It's also essential to consider the training and support provided by the AI tool provider, as this can affect how quickly you can start using the tool and how efficiently you can use it to create content.

It is also important to consider the cost of the AI tool. While some AI tools may seem expensive, they may be worth the investment if they can help you create high-quality content in a more efficient manner. However, it is important to balance the cost of the tool with the potential return on investment (ROI) in terms of time saved and increased content quality.

Another important consideration is the ethics and transparency of the AI tool. It's essential to ensure that the tool's algorithm is not biased and that the AI tool provider has a clear understanding of how the tool works. You should also consider the data privacy implications of using an AI tool and ensure that the provider adheres to all data protection regulations.

Lastly, it's important to evaluate the reviews and feedback from other users who have used the AI tool. Reading reviews from other content creators can provide valuable insights into the tool's strengths and weaknesses, helping you make a more informed decision.

When evaluating AI tools for content creation, it is essential to identify your goals, evaluate the accuracy and user-friendliness of the tool, consider the cost, ethics, and transparency, and review feedback from other users. By considering these factors, you can choose the right AI tool for your content creation needs.

CHAPTER 15 - BEST PRACTICES FOR WORKING WITH AI IN CONTENT CREATION

As we've explored in the previous chapters, AI has a lot of potential in content creation. However, like any technology, there are best practices to follow to maximize its benefits and minimize its risks. In this chapter, we'll discuss some of the best practices for working with AI in content creation.

Know your goals

Before diving into using AI for content creation, it's important to identify your goals. What are you hoping to achieve with AI? Do you want to increase efficiency? Improve accuracy? Enhance creativity? Knowing your goals will help you choose the right AI tools and strategies to achieve them.

Understand the limitations of AI

While AI has many capabilities, it's important to recognize its limitations. AI is not a magic solution that can do everything perfectly. For example, language models may struggle with understanding context or idiomatic expressions, which can lead to inaccurate or nonsensical content. By understanding the limitations of AI, you can use it more effectively and avoid unrealistic expectations.

Choose the right AI tools

There are many AI tools available for content creation, but not all of them will be suitable for your goals and needs. Before selecting an AI tool, consider factors such as its accuracy, compatibility with your workflow, and ease of use. Additionally, be aware of the potential biases and ethical concerns of the AI tools you choose to use.

Train the AI model

In order to get the most out of an AI tool, it's important to train the model with relevant data. This can improve the accuracy and effectiveness of the tool. Additionally, ongoing training can help the AI adapt to changes in your content needs and preferences.

Monitor and evaluate the AI output

While AI can produce high-quality content, it's important to monitor and evaluate its output to ensure that it meets your standards and goals. This can involve reviewing the content for accuracy, relevance, and coherence. Additionally, you may want to track metrics such as engagement and conversion rates to measure the effectiveness of the AI-generated content.

Use AI to enhance human creativity, not replace it

AI can be a powerful tool for content creation, but it's important to remember that it should enhance human creativity, not replace it. AI can automate repetitive tasks and provide suggestions, but it can't replicate the nuance and originality of human creativity. By using AI in combination with human creativity, you can achieve the best of both worlds.

Maintain ethical standards

As with any technology, there are ethical considerations to keep in mind when using AI in content creation. It's important to be transparent about the use of AI-generated content and to ensure that it aligns with ethical standards such as privacy, diversity, and accuracy. Additionally, be aware of the potential biases and limitations of AI models and take steps to mitigate them.

By following these best practices, you can make the most of AI in content creation while minimizing its risks and limitations. Remember that AI is a tool to enhance human creativity, not replace it. With the right approach, AI can help you create high-quality, engaging content more efficiently and effectively than ever before.

CHAPTER 16: COLLABORATING WITH AI: WORKING WITH CHATBOTS AND VIRTUAL ASSISTANTS

Artificial Intelligence has become an integral part of our lives and has revolutionized the way we interact with technology. One of the areas where AI has made significant progress is in chatbots and virtual assistants. Chatbots and virtual assistants have become increasingly popular in recent years, with more and more businesses using them to improve customer service, increase efficiency and reduce costs.

Chatbots and virtual assistants are AI-powered tools that use natural language processing (NLP) to understand and respond to human language. They can perform a wide range of tasks, from answering customer queries to booking appointments and ordering products. By automating routine tasks, chatbots and virtual assistants can free up human agents to focus on more complex issues, improving overall productivity and efficiency.

But working with chatbots and virtual assistants also comes with its challenges. Here are some best practices to keep in mind when collaborating with AI-powered tools:

Define the Scope and Purpose of the Chatbot or Virtual Assistant

Before developing a chatbot or virtual assistant, it's important to clearly define its scope and purpose. This includes understanding what tasks it will be performing, what kind of queries it will be handling, and how it will be integrated with existing systems. By defining the scope and purpose of the tool upfront, you can ensure that it aligns with your business objectives and meets the needs of your customers.

Use a Conversational Tone

One of the key benefits of chatbots and virtual assistants is that they can mimic human conversation. To make the most of this, it's important to use a conversational tone when designing your tool. This means avoiding formal language and jargon and using language that is simple, clear and easy to understand.

Test and Iterate

Like any software development project, building a chatbot or virtual assistant requires testing and iteration. It's important to test your tool with real users to identify any issues or limitations and make improvements based on their feedback. This can help ensure that your tool meets the needs of your customers and is effective in achieving your business objectives.

Ensure Data Privacy and Security

Chatbots and virtual assistants often handle sensitive information such as personal details, payment information and purchase history. It's important to ensure that your tool is designed with data privacy and security in mind. This includes implementing encryption, user authentication, and access controls to protect sensitive information from unauthorized access.

Provide Easy Access to Human Support

While chatbots and virtual assistants can handle many tasks, there will be situations where human intervention is necessary. It's important to provide easy access to human support for these situations. This can include offering a live chat option or providing a clear escalation path for customers who need to speak to a human agent.

Monitor Performance Metrics

To ensure that your chatbot or virtual assistant is meeting its objectives, it's important to monitor its performance metrics. This includes tracking metrics such as response time, customer satisfaction, and task completion rate. By monitoring these metrics, you can identify areas for improvement and make adjustments to ensure that your tool is achieving its intended goals.

Working with chatbots and virtual assistants can be a game-changer for businesses, providing benefits such as increased efficiency, improved customer service, and reduced costs. By following these best practices, you can ensure that your collaboration with AI-powered tools is successful and effective in achieving your business objectives.

CHAPTER 17: AI AND SOCIAL MEDIA – MAXIMIZING ENGAGEMENT

Social media has revolutionized the way we communicate and interact with others. With the rise of platforms such as Facebook, Twitter, and Instagram, we are now more connected than ever before. As businesses and individuals alike seek to leverage the power of social media to engage with their audience, artificial intelligence (AI) has emerged as a powerful tool to help maximize engagement and reach.

In this chapter, we will explore how AI is being used to enhance social media engagement, and provide specific examples of how businesses can leverage AI to drive more interactions and conversions on social media.

Personalized Content Recommendations

One of the most powerful ways that AI is enhancing social media engagement is through personalized content recommendations. By analyzing user data such as search history, page likes, and click behavior, AI algorithms can predict the type of content that users are most likely to engage with and recommend it to them.

For example, YouTube's recommendation system uses AI to analyze user viewing history and offer personalized video recommendations. Similarly, social media platforms such as Facebook and Twitter use AI algorithms to surface content in users' feeds that they are likely to find interesting and engaging.

By leveraging personalized content recommendations, businesses can increase the likelihood that their social media content will be seen by their target audience, leading to increased engagement and conversions.

Automated Chatbots

Another way that AI is being used to maximize social media engagement is through the use of automated chatbots. Chatbots are AI-powered programs that can interact with users in a conversational manner, providing customer service, answering questions, and even making product recommendations.

By using chatbots, businesses can provide quick and efficient customer service, and engage with customers in real-time. This can lead to increased customer satisfaction and loyalty, as well as improved engagement on social media.

For example, H&M uses a chatbot on its Facebook page to help customers find products and answer questions about orders. The chatbot provides a quick and easy way for customers to get the information they need, without having to leave the Facebook platform.

Sentiment Analysis

Another way that AI is being used to enhance social media

engagement is through sentiment analysis. Sentiment analysis involves analyzing social media content to determine the emotional tone of the message.

By using sentiment analysis, businesses can gain valuable insights into how their audience is feeling about their brand, products, or services. This can help them identify areas for improvement, as well as opportunities to engage with customers and improve their social media presence.

For example, Twitter's sentiment analysis tool allows businesses to track the sentiment of tweets related to their brand, and respond to negative feedback in real-time. By addressing customer concerns and feedback in a timely manner, businesses can improve customer satisfaction and build stronger relationships with their audience.

Visual Recognition

Visual recognition is another area where AI is being used to enhance social media engagement. By using visual recognition algorithms, businesses can analyze images and videos shared on social media to identify key objects, scenes, and emotions.

This can help businesses understand how their brand is being represented on social media, and identify opportunities to engage with their audience. For example, a fashion retailer could use visual recognition to identify users sharing photos of their products on social media, and engage with them by offering promotions or discounts.

In addition, visual recognition can be used to identify potential issues or crises before they become major problems. For example, by monitoring social media for images or videos that depict a negative experience with a product or service, businesses can quickly respond to the issue and mitigate any negative impact on their brand.

AI is playing an increasingly important role in maximizing engagement on social media. By leveraging personalized content recommendations, automated chatbots, sentiment analysis, and visual recognition, businesses can improve their social media presence and build stronger relationships with their audience.

The possibilities for using AI to maximize engagement on social media are endless and constantly evolving. As AI technology continues to advance, it will be exciting to see how it will shape the future of social media marketing and the way we connect with our audiences online. By following these best practices and staying up-to-date with the latest trends and developments in AI, content creators can leverage the power of AI to create more effective and engaging social media content.

CHAPTER 18 - LEVERAGING AI IN E- COMMERCE CONTENT CREATION

In today's fast-paced world, e-commerce is becoming an increasingly popular way of shopping for customers. As a result, e-commerce businesses must be able to create high-quality, engaging content that not only showcases their products but also convinces customers to buy them. However, with so many businesses vying for customers' attention, creating such content can be a challenge. Fortunately, advances in artificial intelligence (AI) have made it possible for businesses to create high-quality content quickly and efficiently.

One of the ways businesses can leverage AI in e-commerce content creation is through product descriptions. Traditionally, product descriptions were written by human copywriters, which could be time-consuming and expensive. However, with AI, businesses can use natural language generation (NLG) technology to automatically generate product descriptions. NLG uses algorithms to analyze data and create human-like text. This technology can help businesses create unique and compelling product descriptions that accurately reflect their products and entice customers to make a purchase.

Another way businesses can use AI in e-commerce content creation is through chatbots. Chatbots are computer programs that simulate conversation with human users. They can be used to answer frequently asked questions, provide personalized recommendations, and even process orders. Chatbots can save businesses time and money by handling routine customer inquiries, freeing up employees to focus on more complex tasks. Additionally, chatbots can provide a more personalized experience for customers by tailoring their responses to individual preferences and behavior.

AI can also be used to optimize e-commerce website design. Through machine learning algorithms, businesses can analyze customer behavior on their websites and make data-driven decisions about design and layout. For example, businesses can use AI to analyze which product images and descriptions lead to the most conversions and optimize their website accordingly. AI can also be used to personalize the user experience by analyzing customer behavior and tailoring website content to individual preferences.

In addition to improving product descriptions, chatbots, and website design, AI can also be used to enhance e-commerce marketing efforts. By analyzing customer data, businesses can use AI to create targeted marketing campaigns that are tailored to individual preferences and behavior. For example, businesses can use AI to analyze customer purchase history and create targeted product recommendations or send personalized promotional offers. This can increase customer engagement and loyalty, leading to higher conversion rates and revenue.

However, while AI can be a powerful tool for e-commerce content creation, businesses must also be mindful of potential drawbacks. For example, while NLG can generate high-quality product descriptions, it may not be able to capture the nuances of language that human copywriters can. Additionally, chatbots may not be able to handle complex customer inquiries, leading to frustration and a poor customer experience. Finally, businesses must also be mindful of potential biases in their AI algorithms, which can lead to discrimination and unfair treatment of certain groups.

AI can be a powerful tool for e-commerce businesses looking to create high-quality content quickly and efficiently. By leveraging NLG, chatbots, website design optimization, and targeted marketing campaigns, businesses can improve customer engagement, loyalty, and revenue. However, businesses must also be mindful of potential drawbacks and ensure that their AI systems are designed and implemented ethically and responsibly.

CHAPTER 19 - THE FUTURE OF AI IN CONTENT CREATION

Artificial intelligence (AI) has come a long way in recent years, and it has made significant strides in content creation. From chatbots and virtual assistants to language translation and image recognition, AI has revolutionized the way we create and consume content. As we move towards a future where AI is increasingly integrated into our lives, it's essential to consider how it will shape the world of content creation.

One of the most significant benefits of AI in content creation is its ability to personalize content for individual users. By analyzing vast amounts of data, AI can create tailored content that speaks directly to the user's interests and preferences. This can help content creators build stronger relationships with their audience, leading to increased engagement and loyalty.

In addition to personalization, AI can also help content creators to automate repetitive and time-consuming tasks. For example, AI-powered tools can analyze and optimize SEO, create headlines and summaries, and even generate content from scratch. This can free up time for content creators to focus on more creative and strategic tasks, leading to higher quality content overall.

Another area where AI is having a significant impact is in the realm of visual content. AI-powered tools can analyze and tag images, making it easier to search and categorize visual content. This can be particularly useful for businesses that rely heavily on visual content, such as those in the fashion, beauty, or food industries.

AI is also making it easier to create high-quality visual content, such as graphics and videos. AI-powered tools can generate visuals that are optimized for social media platforms, which can help content creators to increase their reach and engagement. Additionally, AI can also help to improve the accessibility of visual content, by automatically generating alt text descriptions for images and videos.

Despite the many benefits of AI in content creation, there are also some potential drawbacks to consider. One of the most significant concerns is the potential for AI-generated content to be used for malicious purposes, such as the spread of fake news or propaganda. As AI becomes increasingly sophisticated, it's essential to develop safeguards to prevent its misuse.

Another concern is the potential for AI to replace human creativity entirely. While AI can automate many tasks and generate content quickly, it cannot replicate the nuance and emotional depth that humans bring to content creation. As such, it's important to view AI as a tool that can support and enhance human creativity, rather than a replacement for it.

AI has already had a significant impact on content creation, and this is only set to increase in the years to come. By embracing AI as a tool and understanding its potential and limitations, content creators can unlock new levels of creativity and engagement, while ensuring that they are using this powerful technology in a responsible and ethical manner.

CHAPTER 20 - THE HUMAN TOUCH: BALANCING AI AND CREATIVITY IN CONTENT CREATION

Artificial intelligence has made significant strides in content creation, but there's one thing that it can't replace: the human touch. As AI continues to evolve, it's essential to find a balance between utilizing its capabilities and preserving the human element in content creation.

AI can do many things well, including analyzing data, generating reports, and identifying trends. In content creation, AI can assist in tasks such as generating article topics, creating headlines, and even writing short pieces. AI can also analyze user behavior and tailor content to their preferences.

However, AI lacks the ability to understand emotions and context in the same way that humans do. Creativity, empathy, and emotional intelligence are essential elements that only humans can bring to the table. For instance, AI can produce a piece of music or art, but it may lack the emotional depth and personal connection that a human artist could bring.

The key is to find a balance between AI and human creativity. This involves recognizing the strengths and limitations of both AI and humans and using them in combination to produce the best possible content. Humans can bring creativity, emotion, and context to the table, while AI can handle data analysis, content distribution, and other technical aspects.

One example of successful integration of AI and human creativity is in the field of journalism. Many news outlets use AI to generate articles on financial news, sports scores, and even election results. However, human journalists are still responsible for conducting interviews, investigating stories, and providing the context that readers need to understand the news.

Another example is in the film industry. AI can help with tasks such as script analysis and production scheduling. However, the actual filming and directing of a movie requires human creativity and emotional intelligence.

The challenge is to ensure that AI remains a tool for humans to use, rather than replacing human creativity altogether. This requires a commitment to ongoing innovation, collaboration, and experimentation.

One way to maintain the balance is by continuing to educate and train humans to work effectively with AI. This includes understanding how to use AI tools, how to interpret the data they generate, and how to incorporate that data into content creation effectively. By doing so, humans can leverage the power of AI while maintaining their unique creativity and emotional intelligence.

Another way to balance AI and human creativity is by

continually evaluating the results of AI-assisted content creation. This involves monitoring user engagement, analyzing data, and incorporating feedback to ensure that content remains relevant and engaging.

The future of content creation lies in finding the right balance between AI and human creativity. While AI can provide valuable assistance, it's the human touch that brings emotion, context, and creativity to the table. By understanding the strengths and limitations of both AI and humans, we can work together to create content that is both engaging and impactful.

CHAPTER 21: MOST COMMON AI RESOURCES FOR DIGITAL CONTENT CREATORS

Canva - a graphic design tool that uses AI to help users create visually appealing designs

Grammarly - an AI-powered writing assistant that checks grammar, spelling, and punctuation

Hootsuite Insights - a social media analytics tool that uses AI to provide insights and recommendations

Google Analytics - a web analytics service that uses AI to track website traffic and user behavior

Yoast SEO - an AI-powered WordPress plugin that helps optimize content for search engines

Headliner - an AI-powered video editing tool that creates engaging social media videos

Adobe Creative Cloud - a suite of creative tools that uses AI to help users create stunning designs

BuzzSumo - an AI-powered content research tool that helps users discover popular topics and trends

Lumen5 - an AI-powered video creation tool that converts articles into videos

AnswerThePublic - an AI-powered keyword research tool that helps users discover popular questions and queries related to a topic

Zyro - an AI-powered website builder that creates custom websites based on user preferences

SummarizeBot - an AI-powered tool that summarizes text, articles, and web pages

SEMrush - an AI-powered SEO tool that provides insights and recommendations to improve search engine rankings

DeepDreamGenerator - an AI-powered image creation tool that creates unique and surreal images

Wordsmith - an AI-powered writing tool that automatically generates human-like content

HubSpot - an AI-powered marketing automation tool that helps businesses attract, engage, and convert leads

Wibbitz - an AI-powered video creation platform that converts text into engaging videos

Copy.ai - an AI-powered copywriting tool that helps users generate marketing copy and product descriptions

Piktochart - an AI-powered infographic maker that helps users create visually appealing infographics

OBS Studio - an AI-powered live streaming and video recording software

Zest AI - an AI-powered content curation tool that helps users discover and share high-quality content

Post Intelligence - an AI-powered social media management tool that helps users optimize their content for maximum engagement

Article Forge - an AI-powered content creation tool that generates unique articles based on a user's keywords and preferences

IBM Watson - an AI-powered tool that provides natural language processing and machine learning capabilities

Kontentino - an AI-powered social media management tool that helps users plan, create, and schedule content

Canecto - an AI-powered web analytics tool that provides insights and recommendations to improve website performance

Visme - an AI-powered design tool that helps users create infographics, presentations, and reports

Vidyard - an AI-powered video marketing platform that helps businesses create, manage, and analyze video campaigns

CoSchedule Headline Analyzer - an AI-powered tool that analyzes headlines and provides recommendations for improved engagement

Adext - an AI-powered digital advertising tool that optimizes ad campaigns for maximum performance

Cognitiveseo - an AI-powered SEO tool that provides insights and recommendations for improved search engine rankings

Turtl - an AI-powered content creation tool that helps users create engaging and interactive digital content

VWO - an AI-powered website optimization tool that provides insights and recommendations to improve website conversion rates

Phrasee - an AI-powered email marketing tool that generates engaging subject lines and email copy

Unbounce - an AI-powered landing page builder that helps businesses create high-converting landing pages

Persado - an AI-powered marketing tool that generates high-performing marketing messages and content

Wordsmith - An AI tool that automatically generates natural language narratives from data to help content creators quickly generate reports, articles, and other content.

Artisto - An AI-powered video editing app that transforms ordinary videos into animated masterpieces using various filters and effects.

Hugging Face - An open-source library of NLP models and datasets for natural language processing tasks, including sentiment analysis, text summarization, and question-answering.

Copy.ai - An AI-powered tool that generates high-quality marketing copy, product descriptions, and ad headlines with just a few clicks.

Wibbitz - An AI-powered video creation platform that automatically turns written articles into engaging videos.

Lumen5 - An AI-driven video creation tool that allows content creators to turn written content into engaging videos in minutes.

Piction - An AI-powered tool that analyzes written content and automatically creates visual content to complement it.

Artbreeder - An AI art generator that allows content creators to create unique and stunning images by mixing different styles, genres, and media.

Chorus - An AI-powered tool that automatically generates captions and subtitles for audio and video content.

Grid - An AI-powered web design tool that automates the creation of visually stunning websites using AI-generated layouts.

AI POWERED CONTENT CREATION

ContentBot.ai - An AI-powered tool that creates high-quality content, including blog posts, social media updates, and email newsletters.

Vizydrop - An AI-powered data visualization platform that allows content creators to create stunning and interactive data visualizations without any coding.

Sprout Social - An AI-powered social media management tool that helps content creators manage multiple social media accounts, schedule posts, and analyze performance.

Acrolinx - An AI-powered content optimization tool that analyzes written content and provides suggestions for improving its clarity, tone, and style.

Conclusion

The world of content creation is constantly evolving, and one of the most significant changes in recent years has been the integration of artificial intelligence (AI) into the process. From writing and design to distribution and analysis, AI has transformed the way content is created, consumed, and measured. In this book, we have explored the ways in which AI tools can be used by content creators to enhance their work, while also acknowledging the importance of human creativity in the process.

As we have seen, there are a plethora of AI tools available to content creators, ranging from writing assistants and design tools to distribution and analysis platforms. These tools can help content creators streamline their workflow, save time, and improve the quality of their work. However, it is important to note

74

that AI should not be seen as a replacement for human creativity, but rather as a tool to enhance it.

One of the key advantages of AI tools is their ability to automate repetitive tasks, such as keyword research, social media scheduling, and data analysis. This frees up time for content creators to focus on more creative aspects of their work, such as ideation, storytelling, and audience engagement. In addition, AI can help content creators personalize their content to better fit the needs and interests of their audience, thereby increasing engagement and building brand loyalty.

Another advantage of AI is its ability to analyze data and provide insights that can inform content strategy. By tracking metrics such as engagement rates, click-through rates, and bounce rates, content creators can gain valuable insights into what is working and what is not. This allows them to optimize their content strategy and make data-driven decisions about what to create and how to distribute it.

However, while AI has many advantages, it is important to remember that it is not infallible. AI tools are only as good as the data they are fed, and they can sometimes make mistakes or produce results that are biased or incomplete. This is why it is important for content creators to remain actively engaged in the process and to use their own judgment when interpreting data and making decisions.

Ultimately, the most effective content creation process will strike a balance between AI tools and human creativity. By leveraging AI to automate repetitive tasks, personalize content, and analyze data, content creators can enhance their work and improve the overall quality of their content. At the same time, they must continue to rely on their own creativity and expertise to generate fresh ideas, tell compelling stories, and connect with their audience in meaningful ways.

As we move forward into the future of content creation, we can expect to see even more integration of AI tools into the process. However, we must remain mindful of the importance of human creativity and maintain a balance between technology and humanity. By doing so, we can ensure that content creation continues to evolve and improve in ways that benefit both creators and audiences alike.

In conclusion, the integration of AI tools into content creation is an exciting development that has the potential to revolutionize the industry. However, we must be mindful of the limitations and biases of AI, and maintain a balance between technology and human creativity. By doing so, we can create content that is both efficient and effective, while also fostering the unique creativity and expertise of content creators. The future of content creation is bright, and we are excited to see what new developments and innovations lie ahead.

ACKNOWLEDGEMENT

First and foremost I would like to express my profound gratitude to everyone who has contributed to the creation of this book "AI Powered Content Creation : Harnessing the Power of Artificial Intelligence for Social Media." Without your support, expertise and guidance, this project would not come to fruition.

I would like to extend my deepest appreciation to my family, for their unwavering love, understanding, encouragement throught this journey. Your constant support and belief in my abilities have been a driving force behind my pursuit of knowledge and passion for the subject matter.

I would also like to share my gratitude to the experts and professionals in the field of social media and AI who generously shared their knowlege and experiences. I am equally deeply indebted to the reviewers and beta readers who dedicated time and effort to provide valuable feedback and suggestions.

Last but not the least, I would like to express my sincerest thanks to the readers of this book specially those who have also read my previous two books. It is my sincerest hope that the knowledge and insights shared within these pages will inspire you in your journey of leveraging artificial intelligence in the realm of your social media presence.

Thank you. Each and everyone of you for being a part of this endeavor. Your support and contributions have made this book a reality and i am truly grateful.

Lastly, for the love of my life. This book is being published as an eternal gift for your birthday. It is a testament to the inspiration you provide and the actualization of your belief in my abilities.

Eduardo P. Carabeo Jr.

ABOUT THE AUTHOR

Eduardo P Carabeo Jr

Eduardo P. Carabeo Jr is a digital communications expert in content planning, content creation and content curation, copywriting, content analytics audit and review, video editing, and script preparation. So far, he has published two books in Artificial Intelligence.

He has over a decade of extensive experience and high level of proficiency in managing social media accounts in different social media platforms like Facebook, You Tube, Instagram, Tiktok, Printerest, Linked In and Twitter for business accounts. Moreover, he also has over 3 decades of professional experience in actual management - business, office, team, and project management.
One proof of his competency is in my organically grown and operated, monetized You Tube Channel

Splat Communications which has over 4.6M views and over 25K subscribers in a year - with the YT monetization goals achieved in 23 days! The said channel is currently in the Top 1.4% of all other channels in the entire YouTube platform of over 130 million channels globally.
There is no better proof of expertise than this. Link below - Lifetime(1 yr and 3 months) Channel Analytics - 4.5Million Views. Over 358K watch hours, Exceptional Channel Lifetime Click

Through Rate is 10.8%

Aside from his actual experience in Social Media Management, here are other information about the author.
• Completed Social Media Management Course by Meta with a final rating of 94.06%
• Completed Reuter's Digital Journalism Professional program which focuses on the integrity of information and its presentation. Joint project of Reuters and Meta.
• Completed the Google Data Analytics Professional course with a final rating of 92.21%

Former Department Head - Provincial Information Communications Technology office - Marinduque, Philippines

Managing Director at Simplified Strategic Solutions - a business consulting firm

BOOKS BY THIS AUTHOR

The Rise Of Artificial Intelligence : Pivoting To The Knowledge Age

This book is a comprehensive book about Artificial Intelligence. Each chapter is described using non-technical terms to facilitate understanding. It's fully packed with information with everything you want to know about the world of Artificial Intelligence. It's evolution and rise that led to the Knowledge Age we are in right now.

The Ai Adventure : A Hilarious Journey Into The World Of Artificial Intelliigence

Welcome to the wildest and wackiest ride through the world of artificial intelligence you've ever experienced!

This is not your typical, dry as dust academic treatise in AI. No, this is a fun-filled romp through the most exciting and mind-blowing developments in this rapidly evolving field. Aside from understanding what AI IS FOR, you'll also know by heart and in-depth what AI is NOT for.

In these pages, you'll meet the robots, chatbots and cyborgs who are changing the way we live, work and play. You'll learn about the latest breakthroughs in machine learning, natural language processing, and computer vision and how they are being used to revolutionize industries as diverse as healthcare, finance and entertainment.

But this book is not just about the science of AI. It is also about the weird and wonderful ways that humans are interacting with this technology. From asking robots simple questions to creating AI generated art. As a bonus, the pages would contain original and one of a kind AI generated images specially made for this book.

Through it all, you'll be entertained by the slew of quirky AI's. This book is a celebration of the amazing potential of artificial intelligence, and a call to action to ensure that we all harness this power for the good of humanity.

Made in the USA
Columbia, SC
16 September 2024

41134510R00055